JOHN SHINES THROUGH AUGUSTINE

Wipf and Stock Publishers
199 W 8th Ave, Suite 3
Eugene, OR 97401

John Shines Through Augustine
Selections from the Sermons of Augustine
on the Gospel According to Saint John
By Carleton, A. P.
ISBN 13: 978-1-5326-5611-8
Publication date 4/23/2018
Previously published by Association Press, 1959

WORLD CHRISTIAN BOOKS NO. 34

Second Series

JOHN SHINES THROUGH AUGUSTINE

SELECTIONS FROM THE SERMONS
OF AUGUSTINE
ON THE GOSPEL ACCORDING TO SAINT JOHN

translated by

A. P. CARLETON, O.M.B.E.

WIPF & STOCK · Eugene, Oregon

First Series:

(*1*) THE CHRISTIANS' GOD *by Stephen Neill*

(*2*) CHRISTIAN GIVING *by V. S. Azariah*

(*3*) MARK'S WITNESS TO JESUS CHRIST *by E. Lohse*

(*4*) CHRISTIANITY AND SCIENCE *by Charles E. Raven*

(*5*) THE CHRISTIAN AS CITIZEN *by John C. Bennett*

(*6*) THE CHRISTIAN CHARACTER *by Stephen Neill*

(*7*) READING THE BIBLE TO-DAY *by D. T. Niles*

(*8*) JOHN'S WITNESS TO JESUS *by George Appleton*

(*9*) FROM BRAHMA TO CHRIST *by L. Tilak*

(*10*) BEGINNING FROM JERUSALEM *by John Foster*

(*11*) JESUS AND HIS PEOPLE *by Paul Minear*

(*12*) DID JESUS RISE FROM THE DEAD? *by James Martin*

(*13*) THE CROSS IS HEAVEN *by A. J. Appasamy*

(*14*) WHO IS JESUS CHRIST? *by Stephen Neill*

(*15*) A LETTER OF WISE COUNSEL *by E. A. Maycock*

(*16*) RELIGIOUS LIBERTY *by Giovanni Miegge*

(*17*) LIVING WITH THE GOSPEL *by D. T. Niles*

(*18*) LIVINGSTONE IN AFRICA *by Cecil Northcott*

(*19*) CHRIST'S MESSENGERS *by C. F. D. Moule*

(*20*) JAPANESE WITNESSES FOR CHRIST *edited by Norimichi Ebizawa*

(*21*) ONE LORD, ONE CHURCH *by Robert Nelson*

(*22*) THE PEOPLE OF GOD IN THE OLD TESTAMENT *by H. J. Kraus*

(*23*) MATTHEW'S WITNESS TO JESUS CHRIST *by H. N. Ridderbos*

(*24*) THE PSALMS AS CHRISTIAN PRAISE *by R. B. Y. Scott*

Second Series:

(25) PAUL TO THE GALATIANS *by Stephen Neill*

(26) LUKE'S WITNESS TO JESUS CHRIST *by Reginald H. Fuller*

(27) CHRISTIAN PRAYER *by Sister Gertrude, O.M.S.E.*

(28) DESIGN OF MY WORLD *by H. B. Dehqani-Tafti*

(29) THE CHRISTIAN FAMILY *by L. & W. Brown*

(30) KAGAWA, JAPANESE PROPHET *by J. M. Trout*

(31) FAITHFUL WITNESSES *by Edward Rochie Hardy*

(32) MOSES *by Gerhard von Rad*

(33) PALESTINE AND THE BIBLE *by Denis Baly*

(34) JOHN SHINES THROUGH AUGUSTINE *by A. P. Carleton, O.M.B.E.*

CONTENTS

		Page
	FOREWORD BY THE GENERAL EDITOR	8
	INTRODUCTION	9
Chapter		
1	THE FIRST DISCOURSE	14
2	THE SECOND DISCOURSE	26
3	THE THIRD DISCOURSE	31
4	THE FOURTH DISCOURSE	47
5	THE SEVENTH DISCOURSE	50
6	THE EIGHTH DISCOURSE	60
7	THE ELEVENTH DISCOURSE	65
8	THE TWELFTH DISCOURSE	72

This volume is the first of a series in which readers of World Christian Books will be able to hear a number of great voices from the earlier ages of the Church.

Students in the younger Churches say from time to time that they feel themselves nearer to the great Fathers of the Church than to Western teachers of the present day. If this is true, it is good that a certain number of the ancient classics, of various traditions of the Church, should be made easily available for students.

Augustine was a giant of the Western, that is the Latin-speaking, tradition of the Christian faith. It is unlikely that anyone to-day would preach sermons exactly like those from which a number of selections are given in this volume. We have to-day much knowledge which was not accessible to Augustine; and it is right that preachers should make use of this modern knowledge in preparing their sermons and expositions. But perhaps, just because of the difference in outlook and expression, the words of Augustine may help us to go back to the Gospels for ourselves, and to find new ways in which we can experience them as living words of God to us to-day.

Note

Some of the quotations from the Bible in this book are taken from the Revised Standard Version of the Bible; but many others have been exactly translated from the Latin which Augustine used, and which in a number of cases did not very faithfully represent the meaning of the original Latin or Greek.

INTRODUCTION

Most Christians have heard the name Augustine and those who have any acquaintance with the history of the Church know something of his life. His *Confessions* is one of the most famous of books. In it he tells the story of his early life and conversion with such delicate psychological insight that it is not only the most moving of biographies but also a mirror of the ways of man with God. The story of the *Confessions* ends with the return of Augustine, a baptized Christian, already beginning to lead a life of discipline and prayer, to his own country. This was the corner of North Africa now known as Tunisia, but then the Roman Province of Africa.

He settled in a town called Hippo where he was caught up into the life of the Church, first as one of the presbyters, and then at the earnest desire of the people as bishop. The pages which are here translated give us a glimpse of him in those later years as bishop, laying before the people he loved the rich treasures of his new life with God. He had gathered round him a group of devoted disciples who lived in rough houses in the grounds of his house, sharing his life of prayer and dedicating themselves to the special calling of Christ in a life of poverty, chastity and obedience. For these it was his custom to expound the Scriptures day by day, but they were only the nucleus of his audience, for the people of Hippo used to crowd into the large bare basilica which was their church, to hear the teaching of their beloved bishop—by no means only the good and devout, but many who, while refusing to bend their wills in obedience, were willing that their minds should be entertained by the clear thought and brilliant expression of the most powerful intellect of the day. Yet there was no striving for effect or display of learning in his teaching. It was simple and spoke to the heart of man. In many ways it was more informal than the modern sermon. The audience applauded what delighted them, interrupted with questions when they did not understand, and even heckled when they were displeased. The bishop was wonderfully patient with his interrupters, gentle in manner but quick to pick up the weak points and incisive in his replies. In the composition of great sermons the audience has a part to play as well as the preacher. Their interest and eagerness draws out the latent power of the speaker; we should never forget the Hippo congregation in reading the sermons of Augustine.

Augustine was master of the knowledge and learning of his day, and the Latin tongue was a perfect servant to his thought; he knew the Scriptures from beginning to end, and had studied the writings of his predecessors in the Church. But the secret of his power did not lie in these accomplishments. He knew not only what others had said about God, he knew God. That is why he gripped the people of Hippo, and why his words still have power with us.

The surroundings of Augustine were very different from ours. The controversies which rent the Church in Africa have died down. Our education and science are quite different; our text of the Bible is much closer to the original than the ancient Latin translation which Augustine generally used; our methods of exposition are much sounder than the far-fetched allegories that he loved; yet his words speak to our hearts with a freshness and power which the passage of time has not been able to destroy. The secret is this—we learn from him to look up frankly into the face of God. He hides nothing, his trust is complete, and what adoration!

Even those who are familiar with the story of Augustine's life from books of history have seldom read more of his writings than the more interesting parts of the *Confessions*. Even for those who can read Latin—very few in modern days—the sight of a row of folio volumes of closely printed columns is rather discouraging. Translations of many of them can indeed be found in theological libraries, but the treasure is still mainly locked away and few have any idea of what beauty lies hid in those dusty volumes. The inspiration for the preparation of this book came from one who used her knowledge of Latin as a key to unlock the doors of this treasure-house. The study of those heavy volumes became a joy and a source of strength and comfort during the years of a long life as a missionary in India. In old age when all other work had to be laid by, she felt led to share her joy with others. A literal translation on conventional lines in the idiom of the sixteenth century was tried; but it soon became clear that such a translation would be of little more use to the people of to-day than the great Latin folios. Yet, when Augustine preached, Hippo crowded to hear him. How would he speak if English were his language and the people of to-day his audience? What follows is an attempt to answer that question. Much of the original has of necessity been omitted—most of what refers to the controversies and vexed questions of that time, much of the fanciful exposition of the Bible in which his contemporaries took delight and which indeed was

11

often the only way of making any sense of the mistranslations of the old Latin Bible. But the heart of the sermons has been kept, and will be found to have a power that belongs to few religious books of to-day and to communicate a message that has not grown old.

St. Augustine lived, it should be remembered, at a time when an ancient civilization and culture was being overwhelmed by disaster. In A.D. 410, six years before these sermons were preached, Rome itself had been captured and sacked by the uncouth Goths from the North. The structure of the Empire was still intact in the Province of Africa, but its days were numbered. When Augustine lay dying fourteen years later the army of the dreaded Vandals was outside the walls of his city. Like the state, the Church herself was torn and distracted. In Africa a party, working on the native discontent with Roman domination, had built up a separate church organization, bishop against bishop, altar against altar, with ever growing bitterness frequently issuing in violence. These were the Donatists against whom Augustine was compelled to wage a ceaseless struggle. Other controversies tore the Church that remained faithful to the old traditions. The most serious of these is known as the Pelagian controversy, after the British monk Pelagius who set it in motion. Pelagius had reduced the Gospel to little more than a moral system, and seemed to be denying the reality and the power of the grace of God. Grace was the very centre of the experience of Augustine. He threw himself into the controversy with fiery zeal. At times his zeal led him to violence of expression that his friends would forget rather than remember. It was in the midst of all this, then, that his sermons were delivered. He was speaking to ordinary men and women in a world as torn and distracted, as apprehensive of the future, as our own; this is indeed another reason why he has such a living message for us.

St. Augustine's sermons were delivered day after day, with occasional breaks, throughout the year, and form a running commentary on the text of Scripture. But the modern reader will not find them like the commentaries which are written nowadays. St. Augustine does indeed throw wonderful light on the meaning of the Gospel, but there is much more in the sermons than exposition. He is not only explaining the Scriptures; he is bringing the gospel contained in the Scriptures home to his people. He is trying to bring them to God. That is why he breaks away so often from the sequence of the exposition to emphasize some point that they particularly need. Many of these digressions have been omitted from this translation, but even so the reader must be prepared to be carried away from the text of the Gospel to some other subject which seems unconnected.

The translator has not tried to render the full meaning of every word and sentence into English, but to let the great preacher speak to us as he spoke to the people of Hippo. Those who desire the more conventional translation can go to the volumes on the library shelves.

This is, however, real translation, for it is an attempt to accomplish the true purpose of translation. It may not be all that Augustine said, but it is, the translator trusts, Augustine speaking.

CHAPTER ONE

THE FIRST DISCOURSE

How to approach the Gospel

We have just heard in the reading of the Epistle how Paul said, "The natural man cannot receive the things that belong to the Spirit of God" (1 Cor. 2 : 14). As I look round on this large gathering I am inclined to think that there are many "natural" men here— people who are thinking all the time of the things of this world, who cannot lift up their minds to understand the things of the Spirit. And I am here to explain the opening words of the Gospel, "In the beginning was the Word, and the Word was with God, and the Word was God". That is something that no "natural" man will ever understand. Of course I am hesitant. But after all the words were meant to be read, meant to be explained, meant to be understood. And there are at least some among you here who are quite capable of understanding the meaning of the words, who will understand even before I explain them. It would be wrong to deprive them of the teaching they want because others are not fit to receive it. Moreover God of His mercy will give the speaker strength to do his best and the hearers to receive what they can take. For who could really utter this mystery as it ought to be uttered? Could even John do that? John was a man speaking from God, but always a man. He was inspired by God and so able to say something; without God he could have said nothing. But the whole is beyond the

14

power of any man to describe. John could say what he was inspired to say, but he could not say the whole.

You see, my dear brothers, John was one of those mountains mentioned in the Psalm: "The mountains receive peace for thy people, and the (little) hills righteousness" (Psalm 72 : 3). The mountains are the great souls, the hills the lesser ones. The mountains receive peace that the hills may be able to receive righteousness. And that righteousness is what? Faith, because "the righteous lives by faith" (Rom. 1 : 17). The lesser folk would not be able to attain to faith, unless the light of Wisdom like the rising sun shone on the face of the great mountains. So the peace which the mountains receive enables them to reflect the light, in order that the hills may receive as much as they are able to receive and live by faith. The mountains say to the Church, "peace be to you", and in saying it remain one with Him who first gave them peace. So the peace they proclaim is real and not feigned.

You see, my brothers, John had to be a mountain to say, "In the beginning was the Word, and the Word was with God, and the Word was God". What a mountain! How high, towering above the highest peaks, reaching through the cloud-filled vastness, overtopping the highest stars, going up beyond the choirs of Angels in their orders. For if he had not been able to reach beyond the range of all created things, he could never have come to Him through whom all things were made. We can only tell the height of the mountain when we consider the point to which it reaches. Heaven and earth—created things. The things in heaven and earth—all created. Spiritual beings, angels, archangels and all the company of heaven—created. The Psalm mentions them all and then says, "He spoke and they

15

were made: He commanded and they were created" (Ps. 148 : 5). "He spoke"—through His *Word* He created them. John had to pass beyond everything that the Word had made in order to come to "In the beginning was the Word, and the Word was with God, and the Word was God". What a mountain, how holy, how lofty, even among the mountains which receive peace for the People of God that the little hills may receive righteousness!

We may also think of John as one of those mountains we have just sung about in the Psalm: "I will lift up my eyes to the mountains from whence my help will come" (Ps. 121 : 1, 2). So, my brothers, if you wish to understand, lift up your eyes to the mountains; reach out to the writer of the Gospel, try to grasp his meaning. But the mountains *receive* peace. Those who set their hope on men cannot have peace. So do not lift up your eyes to the mountains and at the same time think that you can put your trust in men; for the Psalm goes on, "Our help is in the name of the Lord, who made heaven and earth". So let us lift up our eyes to the mountains from whence our help comes; but let us remember that it is not the mountains themselves in which we must trust. The mountains have received that which they hand on to us. So our trust must there be placed from whence they get their peace. When we lift up our eyes to the Bible, we are lifting up our eyes to the mountains, for the Bible came by the hands of men; but, since they were but men, it was not their own light but a reflected light—the reflection of the true Light that lights up every man that comes into the world (Jn. 1 : 9). John the Baptist was another mountain, and he said, "I am not the Christ" (Jn. 1 : 20). He would run no risk of people trusting in the mountain and falling away from the Light that illuminates the mountain. So he spoke clearly, and said, "We have all received from His fulness" (Jn. 1 : 16). So when you say, "I have lifted up my eyes to the mountains from whence comes my help", do not suppose that the mountain gives the help, but go on to say, "My help comes from the Lord who made heaven and earth".

What I want you to understand, my brothers, is that when you lifted up your hearts to the Scriptures and heard the words of the Gospel, "In the beginning was the Word," and all that follows, you really lifted up your eyes to the mountains. For if the mountains had not spoken, you would have learnt nothing. Help comes to you from the mountains. You hear what they say, but that does not mean that you are able to understand. You must go on to ask the help of the Lord who made heaven and earth. For the mountains are themselves lit up by another light, and only because they have first listened can they speak to us. John who uttered these words was the one who leaned on Jesus' bosom; what he hands on to us he first received from his intimate fellowship with the Master. But what he gives us is words. If you wish for power to understand the words, you must seek it where John himself found what he has given us. When you lift up your eyes to the mountains, you take the cup which is handed to you, (the words of John) but you must do more. To have your heart filled you must go to the well where John drew his water, to Him who made heaven and earth from whom your help comes. I mean that each must lift up his own heart, in his own way, and make a personal effort to grasp what is said.

But you may say that I who am speaking to you am closer to you than God. That is not so. He is much closer to you; for I am present to your sight, He to your mind. Give me your ears and Him your heart, that both may be filled. You lift up your eyes and ears to me, yet not really to me, for I am not one of the mountains, but to the Gospel and its writer; but it is God alone who will fill your hearts. Be careful, however, what you lift up and to whom. Take care what kind of heart you lift up, because you are offering it to the Master. A heart heavy with the lusts of the flesh in attempting to fly upwards will come crashing down. If a man has any such heavy weight hanging round him, he must first get free from it by self-discipline, in order that he may lift up to God a clean heart. "Blessed are the pure in heart, for *they* shall see God" (Matt. 5 : 8).

Words and the Word

"In the beginning was the Word, and the Word was with God, and the Word was God". These are words—are they worth anything at all? That is what we must consider. We are always producing words whenever we open our mouths. Was it such a word that was with God, a word like the words we speak, which sound for a moment and then pass away into silence? If that were all, how could everything be made by Him, and without Him nothing? How, then, could everything be ruled and governed by Him? A Word that is uttered and does not pass away is different from any other word. My dear friends, you must give your minds to this point, for it is very important. We use words every day and they become very cheap. They just sound, and then they are done with—nothing but words. Yet even in man there can be a word that remains in his heart. What comes out of his mouth is sound. The word in his heart has a real existence; you can understand it from the sound you hear, but it is not the sound. For example, when I say, "God", I utter a word—three letters and one syllable. Is this all that God is, three letters and one syllable? Not God, yet think—worthless though that syllable may be, how infinitely precious is the thought that it conveys! Think what happens in your heart when you hear the word "God", what happens in my heart when I say "God". A transcendent reality is brought before the mind which is far above anything in the ever-changing realms of matter and mind. And if I suddenly ask you, Is God liable to change, or is He always the same? you will answer at once, I could never believe in a changeable God or worship Him. God can never change. Your mind, limited in power, tied to the world though it is, could give no other answer: God never changes; His creatures change but never He. How is it that that which is beyond the power of any created mind to understand can so flash upon you that you can answer with complete conviction, God can never change? This is undoubtedly the work of the Word of God in your mind. You know positively and at once that God is alive, everlasting, in complete control, limited by nothing, everywhere present, everywhere whole, no-where confined. When you have thought like this, then you have the word of God in your hearts. Now is that really nothing but the sound of three letters and one syllable? Sounds, syllables and letters are things that pass away. A word, in so far as it is sound, floats away on the air; but as far as it is thought in the mind of the man who thinks and speaks, and in the mind of the man who hears and understands, it abides, though the sounds pass away.

Think a little more about this kind of word. You can have a word in your mind which is like a child of your own heart, an idea conceived and ready to be brought forth into the world. Everything that is accomplished in the world, for instance any great work of architecture, begins with an idea conceived in the mind. The idea is there, but the work has yet to be done. The architect can see what it is going to be, but no one else can have any idea of the grandeur of it, until he starts to build something that can be seen and brings the whole construction to perfect completeness in all its parts. Then people will be lost in wonder at what they see, and come to love what they cannot see, the creative thought in the mind of the architect.

If a fine building makes us appreciate the mind of the man who designed it, what of the mind of God which is Jesus Christ the Master—the Word of God? Study the works of the Word. From them you can form some idea of what the Word is like. Consider how this created and visible world has been constructed. Consider its complementary parts, the heavens and the earth. What words are adequate to express the wondrous beauty of the sky or the profusion that springs up from the earth? Who can adequately describe the changes of the seasons or the power that lies in a seed? What need is there to say more on this theme? Your thoughts can run faster than my words. From all this perfection of structure you can form some idea of the Word through whom it was all made. And all this is still only a part. These are the things you can see or touch. The Word also made the angels, archangels and all the orders of spiritual beings. When you try to imagine what the Word is like, you must take these creatures of His into account as well.

Someone among my hearers may want to ask, Whose thought does this Word express? You must not think of anything common or ordinary when you hear of the WORD, and confuse it with the words you use every day. "These are the words he used", "These words were said", "I got these words from you"—continual turning over of words makes them seem of little value. But when you hear, "In the beginning was the Word," shake yourself free from your ordinary notions about words, and listen to the truth you are to ponder: "The Word was God".

Dare any Arian[1] stand up and say, The Word of God was created? How could that Word be created, when God created all things through Him? You would have to look for another Word behind the Word to account for its existence. And remember, by the Word we mean the one and only Son of God. If you grant the absurdity of another Word behind the Word, then admit that He through whom all things were made was Himself not made. He who made all things could not have been made by Himself.

It is better to believe what the Evangelist has said. He could easily have said, "In the beginning God made the Word", just as Moses said, "In the beginning God made heaven and earth". There we read again and again, "God said, Let it be made, and it was made"—all the various kinds of created things (Gen. 1). What comes between God who speaks and the creation that is made, what mediates the creation? The Word, because He *spoke* and it was made. This is the Word that cannot change. Everything created by Him is subject to change, but He remains unchangeable.

[1] Arians were the followers of Arius, who at the beginning of the fourth century had put forward what he considered a rational form of the Christian faith. He was willing to accept the Word as the highest of created beings, "a second God", but not as being God Himself. His doctrine was condemned at the Council of Nicaea in A.D. 325.

The Word re-creates

There is a further thought. The Word not only creates, He recreates. If you have wrong notions about the Word in His capacity as Creator and defective faith in Him, what sort of idea will you have of the Word as the restorer of His creation, and what hope will there be of your being re-made by Him? Your making was His work, your failure your own. Your restoration cannot be effected by yourself, only by Him who originally made you. You must have a worthy idea of the Word if you wish to be re-created by Him. The Evangelist says, "In the beginning was the Word". Are we going to say, "In the beginning God created the Word"? He could have said the latter, but he did not. The Word was not made, HE WAS, that the truth might stand firm that everything was made by Him and without Him nothing. "In the beginning was the Word, and the Word was with God, and the Word was God". If you cannot understand how this could be, then wait a little, give yourself time to grow. The Word is food for the full grown. Drink your milk now, and then you will grow strong to take that more solid food.

All things

"All things were made through Him, and without Him nothing was made". Sin was not made by Him, but then sin has no positive existence, it is a negative thing, and those who sin are bringing their own life to nothing. But everything that really exists, every created being, the stars shining in the sky, the birds flying in the air, the creatures moving on the ground, absolutely all of them from the angel to the maggot, are His making. The angel is made for heaven and the worm for the earth. God has made both and put them in their right place. The greater creatures and the lesser ones, things above and things below, spiritual beings, beings living in bodies, all are made by Him. There is no pattern of life, no combination of elements, no organism, no substance, nothing that can be weighed, counted or measured, that has not been put in order by the Word who created it, as it is said, "By measure, number and weight thou didst order all things" (Wisdom 11 : 20).

Life

Now comes the question, How were all things made by Him? "All things were made through Him, and without Him was made nothing that was made. In Him was Life". The words could be rendered, "What was made in Him is life", which would mean that everything is life, earth is life, wood is life, stone is life. This would involve us in the belief that there is a soul in inanimate things. Indeed there is a sect that holds these views, the Manichees, and they quote these words in proof. But this is not the right interpretation. The words "In Him was life" are the beginning of a new sentence. The earth is created, but the created earth is not life. Rather, there is in the supreme Wisdom a spiritual principle, through which the world was made. This thing is life.

My dear friends, I must do my best to explain this. A carpenter makes a box, but first he sees the design of the box in his mind. If he had not had the idea, he could never have made the article. But the idea of the box in his mind is not the box you see with your eyes. As long as it exists in idea you cannot see it; only when it is given material form do you see it. But when it is made, does it cease to exist in idea? It exists in both ways, as an idea in the mind and as an article which actually exists. The material box can rot away, and another can be made from the idea which continues to exist in the mind of the maker. Mark the difference between the idea of the box and the box. The box is not life, but the idea of the box is, because the mind of the craftsman, where the box was before it gained concrete shape, is a living thing. In the same way, my dear brothers, the Wisdom of God, through whom all things were made, held all things in idea before He made them. So the things that are produced by the idea are not themselves life, but they have the life only in so far as they are related to Him. You see the earth: there is also an idea of the earth. You see the sky: there is an idea of the sky. In so far as they are visible, they are only bodies; in so far as they are related to the idea, they are life.

Do your best to understand this. It is a deep thought; but it does not come from any profundity of my mind, but from a Mind that is truly great. These thoughts could not have come out of my little mind, but His mind is not little to whom I look to get my inspiration. We must each take what we are capable of receiving, and if this is too much for you now, you must let your mind grow so as to be able to grasp it some day. If you cannot manage adult food, start on milk. Hold fast to Christ, the Man born in this world, if you wish to come to Christ, begotten of the one Father, the Word of God who is with God, through whom all things were made; for real life is that which in Him is made the light of men.

Light
This is what he goes on to say, "And the life was the light of men". Men are lit up by the life—men, not

animals, for animals do not possess the mental powers which make the acquisition of wisdom possible. But man was made in the image of God, and does possess these mental powers. So the life, through which all was made, is the light of *men*, as he says lower down, "The true light was there, which illuminates every man that comes into the world". John the Baptist was lit up by this light, and so was John the Evangelist. He who could say, "I am not the Christ, but there is One who comes after me the lace of whose shoe I am not worthy to untie", was bright with that light; and so was he who could say, "In the beginning was the Word, and the Word was with God, and the Word was God". That is the true Light of men.

But it may be that some hearts, heavy with sin, are too dull to receive the light or even to know that it is there. Because of their sin they are made darkness, and have no idea that they have no light. "The light shines in the darkness, and the darkness did not comprehend it". It is as though a blind man were to stand in the sunlight. He is in the presence of the sun, but he does not know that he is. The stupid man who lives in sin rejecting God is just as blind in heart. Wisdom is there, but if the man is blind it might just as well not be there. The barrier is not in the Wisdom but in the heart. What must he do? He must purify his heart to see God. When a man's eyes are so inflamed with dirt or smoke that he loses his sight what does the doctor say? Wash the dirt out of them and then you will see. Sins and misdeeds are like the smoke and the dirt. God is the true Wisdom, and is not far away from us; if we wish to see Him, then we must wash out the sin from our hearts—"Blessed are the pure in heart, for they shall see God" (Matt. 5 : 8).

CHAPTER TWO

THE SECOND DISCOURSE

Dear friends, what a joy and privilege it is for us to be able to explore the Holy Scriptures, and especially the Holy Gospels, leaving nothing out; to take from them as much as we can find to feed our life, and then to pass on the treasure for you to share.

The Word and a Man

Last Sunday, we studied the first verses of the Gospel: "In the beginning was the Word, and the Word was God, etc." Now we come to, "There was a man sent from God whose name was John". What a contrast! First the description of Christ's mysterious existence as God beyond the capacity of our minds to understand, and then a man on earth with a name.

In the beginning *was* the Word—eternal existence— He is that, always that, never changing, always absolute existence, the "I am that I am" who revealed Himself to Moses. Everything else is completely different; everywhere is change. Every physical organism is born, grows up, grows old and dies. The human mind is similar, for character is always changing under the influence of its own varying inclinations. Who can grasp, however much he put his mind to it, the truth that there is One who never changes, One who is?

A traveller looks from far away at his home across the water. He sees where he has to go, but he has no way of getting there. So we see far away our eternal home where He who is simply is without any change; but the broad sea of this world through which we are going lies in front of us. We can just see the place; some cannot even do that; but there is no way of going across. So He who is where we desire to go came over to us to provide a means for us to pass over. How can we go across water but on wood—the wood of His cross? That is the only means of getting across the sea of this world. Even the blind can clasp this cross. Even the person who cannot see from afar where he is going can grasp that wood, and hold tight to it. It will bring him to his home.

The Cross of Christ

I want to get this thought into your minds, my dear friends, that the secret of a real Christian life is to take hold of Christ in the form in which He came to us, in order that we may come to Him as He is and always has been. He came for the very purpose that He might become our means of transport, to bring us across the water to our home where no more boats are needed because there is no more sea to cross. It is very much better to have no vision of eternal reality and to stay close to the cross than to have a clear mental picture of ultimate existence and to despise Christ crucified for us. It is even better still—best of all, both to see the end and to hold fast the means.

The great "mountains" who were enlightened with the light of righteousness had minds great enough to see that which *is*. John saw the vision and wrote, "In the beginning was the Word". They saw; yet they did not let go the cross or feel ashamed of the lowliness of Christ. The lesser folk who cannot see the vision can hold fast to the sufferings and resurrection of Christ

and so cross the sea in the same boat as those othe
who saw the vision.

The rejection of humility

Religious thinkers of this world have sought for the
Creator through the creation. Paul tells us that it is
quite possible to do this: "From the way the world is
made the invisible nature of God is clearly understood
from created things—namely His moral character
that never changes and His Godhead. And this takes
from them every excuse". Then he goes on, "Because,
although they knew God . . .". He does not say "Because
they did not know God". Because, although they knew
God, they did not glorify Him as God or thank Him,
but became vain in their thoughts, and their senseless
heart was darkened. How was it darkened? He gives
the reason clearly, "Saying they were wise they became
fools". They could see where to go, but forgetting to
thank Him who gave them the vision, they came to
think that it was their own achievement. In this conceit
they lost the vision, turned to idols, and worshipped
beings created like themselves despising their Creator.
This was their final depravity, the working out of their
pride—they claimed to be wise. They had known God,
they had seen what John proclaimed, that all things
were created by the Word of God. These truths are
found in their books, even the truth that there is an only
Son of God by whom all things exist. They had had the
vision—from very far off perhaps, but still the vision;
but they did not want to hold fast to the humility of
Christ, the only boat that would take them safely
across the sea to that distant vision. The cross of Christ
disgusted them.

Conceited wisdom! There is the sea to cross and the

boat is not good enough! You laugh at Christ on the cross: yet He is that one whom you saw from far off, the Word that was in the beginning with God. Why was He crucified? Because you needed the wood of His humility. You, stuck up with pride, you will never cross the broad sea that lies across your road except on a boat of wood. Thankless creature, to despise Him who came to take you across! He came to be the Way, the path through the sea. Did He not walk on the sea to show that it could be crossed? (Matt. 14 : 25). But you cannot walk on the sea, you must get into the boat—believe in Him who was crucified and you will arrive at your goal.

God comes as Man

He was crucified for you, to teach you to be humble. If He had come as God, no one would have been able to know Him. Those who could not see God could not have seen Him either. In so far as He is God, it is not His way to come and go, for He is present everywhere, yet contained in nothing. In what manner did He come? He came as man.

God came hidden in a man. So another man of great spiritual stature had to come to tell people that He was more than man. And so the Gospel goes on, "There was a man". How could he tell the truth about God? We read on, "Sent from God". What was he called? "Whose name was John". Why did he come? "He came for the purpose of witness, to bear witness to the light, that all might believe through him". What kind of man was this? a great man—great in God's sight, great by God's grace, towering above all others; yet he was only a "mountain", a mountain that is all dark until the rising sun throws a vesture of light around it. Pay

attention to what follows: "He was not that light".
If you lose sight of that, you will find John not a
mountain to strengthen you, but a rock in the sea to
wreck you. Look beyond the mountain to Him who
lights up the mountain, for the mountain is there for
this purpose only that it may first catch the light and
bring you the news that the sun has risen.

The real light

"John was not that light". For what purpose did he
come? "To bear witness to the light". To what intent?
"That all men might believe through Him". What
light did he witness to? "That was the real light".
Why "real"? Because there is original light and
reflected light. John was light but not the real light.
Alone he is darkness, placed in the light he becomes
light. It is the same with all men; as Paul says, without
God they are darkness; but when they believe they are
light: "You were once darkness but are now light in the
Lord". The last words are the important ones, "In the
Lord". In yourselves you are darkness; in the Lord you
are light. That is the meaning of "He was not that
light, but was sent to bear witness to the light". Where
was the real light? "There was a real light that lights
up every man that comes into the world", and that
Light is the revealed Word.

CHAPTER THREE

THE THIRD DISCOURSE

The Law and the Gospel

It is hardly necessary to remind you, dear friends, that you are Christians and therefore belong to Christ. We carry His sign on our foreheads, and if we also carry it in our hearts we shall never be ashamed to own Him. The sign speaks of His lowliness. The Lord gave a star bright and shining in the sky as a sign to the Wise Men, but when He put a sign on our foreheads it was not the star but the cross. The instrument of His humiliation is the sign of His glory, and His way of lifting up those who are willing to be lowly. We belong to the Gospel, to the New Testament. "The Law was given by Moses, grace and truth came by Jesus Christ". Ask the Apostle and he will tell you that you are not under law but under grace: "He sent His own Son, made of a woman, made under the law, to bring back those who were under the law, that we might be adopted as sons". This is the very purpose for which Christ came.

Then who gave the Law? The very same Person who gave grace, but He sent the Law by His servant and came down Himself with grace. How did men come to be under the Law? By failing to keep the Law. A man who fulfilled the Law would not be under it, but in complete harmony with it; but he who has fallen under the law is not lifted up by it, but crushed down by it. The Law makes men realize this: it does not remove their sin, but shows them what sinners they are.

The Law tells you what to do, the Giver of the Law understands your difficulty in doing it. Men try to fulfil the Law by their own power. Down they come in their self-confidence and find themselves not masters of the Law but its prisoners. When they realize the condition they are in, then they start begging someone to help them get free. The Law has touched the spring of their pride. Once sick and too proud to admit it, they now find the humility to confess their illness. Now that they admit that they are sick, they plead that the doctor may come and cure them.

Christ Crucified

Who is this Doctor? No other than our Lord Jesus Christ, whom men saw in this world, even the men who did Him to death on the cross—who was arrested, insulted, flogged, spat upon, crowned with thorns, hung on a cross; who died, whose body was pierced with a spear, taken down from the cross and laid in a tomb. This Jesus and no other is our Doctor, completely competent to deal with our wounds. They mocked Him, shook their heads at Him, saying, "If you are the Son of God come down from the cross". Why did He not show His true nature as Son of God, when they challenged Him? Because He could not come down from the cross? He who rose from the dead could certainly have come down from the cross. He suffered all the insults because He had embraced the cross not as a proof of power but as an example of patience. He cured your wounds in the long drawn-out pain of His own. By His willingness to suffer death at a point in time He set you free from the doom of eternal death. He died; or should we rather say that death died in Him? What a death it was that slew death!

Who is He?

Was it really our Lord Jesus Christ who was seen, and touched, and crucified, the whole of Him? Yes, but it was not the whole of Him that the Jews saw. What was it that they could not see? "In the beginning was the Word". The beginning of what? "The Word was with God". What kind of word? "The Word was God". Made by God? No, for "He was in the beginning with God". Then everything that God made was different from the Word? Exactly, for "all things were made through Him, and without Him nothing was made". How made through Him? "With regard to what was made, in Him was life". Life was there before anything was made. What was made was not life, but life was there in idea, in the Wisdom of God, before anything was made. What is made passes away: what exists in the divine Wisdom cannot pass away. So there was life in what was made. What kind of life? Physical life which comes to an end with the life of the body? No, for "the Life was the light of men". Not of animals? In a sense animals too are illuminated, but the light of men is a special thing; for there is a vast difference between men and animals, not in body but in mind. You have nothing else to boast of; animals can be stronger than you are; flies can move faster; you have nothing to compare with the peacock's tail. In what are you superior? You are made in the image of God.

Where is that image to be found? Evidently in the powers of your mind, your understanding. You are different from the animals because you have a mind beyond the range of theirs. The light of man is the light of his mind. The light of the mind is something beyond the mind, something greater than all minds put together. This was the Life through whom all things were made.

Light and Darkness

Where was it? Here, or with the Father and not here? Or is it truer to say, With the Father and still here? If here, then why not seen? Because "the light shines in the darkness, and the darkness will not understand it". Man, refuse to be darkness! Refuse to be faithless, unjust and unfair, greedy and grasping, a lover of the world. That is what darkness means. Not that the Light is not there, but you have shut yourselves away from the light. The blind man stands in the sun but he does not see the light, it might not be there as far as he is concerned. Refuse to be darkness! This is the grace that I am going to talk about, that we are no longer to be darkness, as Paul says, "You were once darkness but are now light in the Lord". As this light was not physical light but the light of the mind, it was necessary that there should be a person, himself not darkness but full of light, to bear witness of the light. To say that he was full of light does not mean that he was himself the light. "He was not that light, but came to bear witness to that light". What was that light? "It was the true light that illuminates every one that comes into the world". Where was it? "He was in the world". How in the world? In the same way as the light of the sun and the moon and the stars are in the world? No, for "the world was made by Him and the world knew Him not". In other words, "The light shines in the darkness and the darkness understood it not". The dark world is the society of those who love the world. It was not the created *things* that did not know their Creator. The sky gave witness in the star (Matt.

34

2 : 2); the sea gave witness when it supported the Christ as He walked on it (Matt. 14 : 25); the winds gave witness, when at His command they were still (Matt. 8 : 27); the earth gave witness, when it quaked at the crucifixion (Matt. 27 : 51). These all knew Him; only those whose hearts were set on the world they loved failed to recognize Him. The world is evil because evil men live in it, just as a house is called bad not from its walls, but because those who live in it are bad.

Sonship

"He came to his own, and his own did not receive Him". How hopeless it would be if we could not read on, "To as many as received Him He gave power to become the sons of God". Sons—then they must have been born, but how? "Who were born, not of blood, nor of the will of the flesh, nor of the will of man, but of God". What an amazing privilege that sonship, and what joy to possess it! And the title deeds to prove it? "And the Word was made flesh and dwelt among us". That was the medicine, made of the same stuff as those whom it healed. Restored to health what did we see? "We saw His glory, the glory as of the only-begotten Son of the Father, full of grace and truth".

Grace

John bore witness about Him and cried saying, "This is He of whom I spoke, He who comes after me existed before me, because before me HE WAS". That is what John says of Him. Listen to what He says of Himself, "Before Abraham was, I AM" (Jn. 8 : 58); and again to what the Father says of His Son, "I begat thee before the morning star" (Ps. 110 : 3).[1] He who is the Light that gives light to everything that can receive light must have been there before them all.

Then he goes on, "And of his fulness we have all received—grace for grace". First He gives us out of His fulness grace, and then more grace. That first grace which we receive, what is it but faith? Walking in faith is walking in grace.

What had we done to deserve this? Turn over the things hidden in your heart and take stock of them, not just asking what you have got there, but how it came to be there. You will find that your efforts deserve nothing but punishment. If you deserved to be punished, and someone came, not to punish you but to forgive you, what you received was a free bounty and not something that you had a right to because you had earned it. That is what grace means, something that is freely given, undeservedly received. The first grace that the sinner receives is the forgiveness of his sins. Has he deserved it? What does justice say? "Punish him". What does mercy say? "Freely forgive him".

This was all promised by the prophets, so that when Christ came He might bring not only grace but truth—truth, because God's promises had come true.

"Grace for grace". Let us go into this more closely. By faith we are brought into fellowship with God; and since we in no way deserved to have our sins forgiven, that faith which brought us this undeserved bounty is itself called grace. What does grace mean? That which is given gratis, free and for nothing—given and in no way earned. God did not *have* to give it—we had no right to it like wages. If you had earned it, that would

---

[1] Augustine is here using the old Latin version of the Psalms; a different rendering will be found in the R.S.V.

have implied that you were good. But, in fact, you were bad, so you believed Him who "justifies the ungodly" (Rom. 4 : 5). What does that mean? It means that God takes a bad man and makes him good. Think what you deserved by law and what you got by grace. You got faith, and by faith you became "righteous", as Paul says "The righteous lives by faith" (Hab. 2 : 4; Rom. 1 : 17). God is pleased with you, when you live by faith; so the reward of immortality and eternal life is yours. That too is grace. For what merit of yours do you get eternal life? You get it by grace. If faith is grace, and eternal life is as it were the reward of faith, you might think that God gives eternal life as something that we have earned. But as the original faith is "grace", so the eternal life is "grace for grace".

So Paul speaks both of the grace he has received and the reward he hopes for. Of the grace he says, "I who was formerly a blasphemer and a persecutor and an inflicter of injury—I obtained mercy" (1 Tim. 1 : 13). He does not say that he got it because he deserved it, but because God was good. Then in another place he claims his reward: "For I am about to be offered, and the time of my departure is at hand. I have fought the good fight, I have finished my course, I have kept the faith; for the rest there is laid up for me a crown of righteousness". He lays claim to it; and note what follows, "which the Lord, the just Judge, will give me in that day" (2 Tim. 4 : 6–8). To get grace he needed a merciful Father, to get the reward of grace a just Judge. Will He who did not condemn him when he was ungodly condemn him when he is full of faith?

If you think it out, you will see that it is not that you have done anything to deserve it, but He has given you the faith which makes you worthy of it. When He gives you the gift of immortality He crowns His own bounty, not your deserts. So then, brothers, "from His fulness" —the fulness of His mercy, the abundance of His generosity—"we have all received". Received what? Forgiveness of sins that we might be justified by faith. And then what? "Grace for grace". We live in grace by faith, and then we receive a further something, which is nothing else than more grace which we have done nothing to deserve. So God crowns in us the gifts that He has given us in His mercy on one condition, that we go on walking in the grace that we first received.

The Law

"For the Law was given by Moses"—that made us guilty. Did not the Apostle say, "The Law came that the transgressions of the law might abound"? (Rom. 5 : 20). The Law is the right treatment for the proud; it shows how many faults they have. They had a high opinion of their own capacity and powers, but they found that they could not do one thing right without the help of Him who gave the Law. God would bring down this pride by giving the Law, saying in effect, "Try keeping this; and do not imagine that there is no Law-giver. What is lacking is not the Law-giver; what is lacking is anyone who fully keeps the Law".

But, if no man has ever fully kept the Law, what is the cause of this? Just this, that sin and death were passed on to him when he was born. Born into the race of Adam he inherited the effects of his fall, the unhealthy desires of man's lower nature. Another man had to be born without that inheritance of wrong desire. There is man and the Man; one brings death, the Other life. So the Apostle tells us: "Since by man came death by man came also the resurrection of the dead".

Who brought death and who resurrection? (1 Cor. 15 : 21, 22). Be patient, and read on: "As in Adam all die, so in Christ shall all be made alive." Who belong to Adam? All who are born of Adam. Who to Christ? All who are born through Christ. Why are all born in sin? Because no one is born outside the race of Adam. Men are born in Adam whether they like it or not, and are all under sentence of death. Birth through Christ is a matter of free will and grace. No one is compelled to be born of Christ: there is no choice in being born of Adam. All born of Adam are sinners born in sin. All born of Christ—God treats them as righteous and makes them righteous, not for their own merits but for Christ's. How? Because our Head, the Lord Jesus Christ, came into the world free from the heritage of sin, yet with a real human nature.

The Lord's Death

Death was the punishment of sin; but the Lord's death was not punishment; it was something He gave us out of His compassion. The Lord had done nothing to deserve death. He said, "Behold the prince of this world comes and has nothing in me". Why then, Lord, did you die? He goes on to tell us: "But that all men may know that I do the will of my Father, arise, let us go out" (Jn. 14 : 30, 31). He had done nothing to deserve it, yet He died. You have done plenty to deserve it, and you object to dying! Do not hesitate to bear with a calm mind that which you deserve, for He did not hesitate to bear it to save you from eternal death. There is man and Man; but one is nothing more than man, the other is God-man. One is the man of sin, the other the Man of righteousness. You died in Adam. Rise in Christ! You have a debt to pay to both. You have believed in Christ; yet you must pay what you owe in Adam. The chain of sin cannot hold you for ever; for the death of the Lord once accomplished in time has pronounced the death sentence on your eternal death. That is Grace, brothers, and that is Truth too, for it was promised and has been fulfilled.

It is not found in the Old Testament, because the Law could warn you but it could not help you; it could command you, but not heal you; it could show up your weakness, but not remove it. But it did prepare you to receive the visit of the Doctor with His medicine of grace and truth. It is the dresser He sent ahead to do the first aid. The patient was not well, he did not want to get well, and told everyone that he was well. Along came the Law and put on the bandages. He then realized how ill he was and complained that the bandages hurt. Along came the Lord with His medicines strong and bitter. He tells the patient, Take it patiently; endure; do not love the world; be patient; let the fire of self-control cure you; let your wounds bear to feel the sharp knife of persecution. You are frightened because you are bound up. Christ was not bound; freely He took the medicine which He gives you. He died for you, so that He might be able encouragingly to say to you, "Are you afraid to suffer for yourself when I first suffered for you?" That is what grace is—grace abundant. Who can adequately extol it?

I am speaking of Christ in His lowliness, my brothers; who is able to describe Him as God in His glory? Even as it is, how inadequate my words are! I cannot give all you want to know, only some food for thought. Think for yourselves about the lowliness of Christ. Do I hear someone saying, Who can explain all this to us, if you do not do it? There is Another speaking to you in your heart. The voice of one who lives in the house is better than the voice of him who shouts from the street. *He* has taken up His residence in your hearts; *He* can show you the grace of His humility. The truth is that until we are able to understand His humility we shall never be able to understand His majesty. If "the Word was made flesh" is too much for us, how can we come to understand "In the beginning was the Word"? My brothers, hold on where you have found firm ground under your feet.

The Law and the Gospel

"The Law was given by Moses, Grace and Truth came by Jesus Christ". The Law was given by a servant and held men guilty, forgiveness was given by the King and set them free. As a servant Moses did not take upon himself more than a servant's part. Because he was faithful in God's house, he was chosen for a great task, but only as a servant. He could act within the Law, but not set men free from the guilt that the Law had brought upon them. "The Law was given by Moses, Grace and Truth came by Jesus Christ".

In case anyone should raise the objection, "How could grace and truth fail to come by Moses, who had seen God?", he goes on to say "No man has seen God at any time". How then did God make Himself known to Moses? As a master makes himself known to his servant. Who was the Master? Christ Himself, who first sent the Law by a servant, intending Himself to come with grace and truth. No one has ever seen God; but this servant saw his Master as far as he was capable of seeing. But how was this done? He tells us: "But the only begotten Son who is in the bosom of the Father, He declared Him". "In the bosom": what does that mean? Of course it does not mean that God was sitting in a chair with the copious folds of His dress spread out to take His children in His lap. It denotes the most intimate relationship between the Father and the Son. He could proclaim the Father because He knew Him as a Son. No man had ever seen God; so He came to tell what *He* had seen. What then did Moses see? A cloud, an angel, fire—but these are all created things. He saw, not a direct vision, but symbols. You tell me, Is not it clearly written that "Moses talked with God face to face as a man with his friend"? True, but if you read on you will find Moses saying, "If I have found grace in thy sight, show me thy face openly that I may see thee". God's answer was, "You cannot see my face" (Ex. 33 : 11, 13, 20). So then, my brothers, the angel who talked with Moses was a symbol of the Lord, and all that was done by the angel pointed forward to the grace and truth that was coming. This is obvious to those who have studied the Law, and we shall use this opportunity to explain it to you as far as the Lord has enabled us to understand it.

How can we see God?

You must understand that those bodily appearances were not God, they were quite different from God. How can God be seen? Turn to the Gospel. "Blessed are the pure in heart, for they shall see God" (Matt. 5 : 8). There have been foolish people who have said that the Father is the invisible God and the Son the visible. The Son certainly became visible, but that was only when He took human nature. Even then, when men were able to see His human form, only some believed, the others crucified Him. Even those who had believed faltered when He was crucified, and only by touching Him after His resurrection did they get their faith back. After the Incarnation the Son was visible; that we admit, for it is the faith of the whole Church. But that He was visible before the Incarnation—only one who is crazy could make such a mistake as that. The visions seen before the Incarnation were physical things created by God and used as symbols of the reality that could not be seen. A simple line of proof will make this clear. You cannot see the Wisdom of God with your eyes. My brothers, if Christ is the Wisdom of God and the Power of God (1 Cor. 1 : 24), if He is the Word of God, how can you expect to see God's Word when you cannot even see man's word?

The Spirit of the Law

If you would really be under grace and belong to the New Testament you must clear your mind of ideas that belong to a lower stage of development. The New Testament claims to give us eternal life. Turn to the Old Testament and you will find that the commandments given to a people in a low state of moral development apply to us also. We are just as much bound to worship only one God. So too the commandment not to take God's name in vain. The commandment to keep the sabbath is even more exacting for us, for we have to keep it in spirit. It was enough for the Jews to keep the letter; there was nothing to stop them flirting or getting drunk on the sabbath. It is very much better for women to be busy inside with their spinning than to be dancing on the verandas in full view of anyone in the street. We are forbidden to do menial work on the sabbath, but what does this mean? What is menial work? It is *sin*. Our Lord tells us that he who commits sin is the slave of sin (Jn. 8 : 34). Sin is then the menial work from which we have to abstain on the sabbath.

We have to keep all the commandments, but what is offered us for doing so? In the Old Testament various rewards are promised such as victory in battle, possession of the promised land (Lev. 26 : 1–13). People who were incapable of grasping the invisible had to be drawn by what they could see; otherwise they might slip back into idolatry. And this is exactly what happened. They forgot the amazing miracles that God had done before their eyes—the crossing of the sea and the drowning of their enemies (Ex. 14 : 21–31)—and as soon as Moses the man of God was out of sight they were off after their idols: "Make us gods to go before us, for that man has left us". Their whole mind had been set on man and not on God. If the man had died, was the God who had led them out of Egypt dead too? So they made an image of a calf and worshipped it and said, "These are your gods, Israel, who delivered you from Egypt" (Ex. 32 : 1–4). How quickly they forgot the grace that had been so openly shown! What other motive could draw such people than material rewards?

Eternal Life

The same commandments apply to us as to them, but not the same promises. What is promised to us? Eternal Life. "This is eternal life that they should know thee the one true God and Jesus Christ whom thou hast sent" (Jn. 17 : 3). It is promised that we should know God—"grace for grace". Brothers, at present we do not see, we believe. Our faith will be rewarded by the sight of its object. The Prophets knew this, but it did not become clear until Christ came. It was hunger of love that inspired the Psalmist when he

44

said, "One thing I desired of the Lord and I will go on asking for it". What was it? A promised land flowing with milk and honey? Victory in war, revenge upon enemies, power and influence in the world? Just listen. "That I may live in the house of the Lord all the days of my life". Imagine that you are dwelling in the house of the Lord. What will be the source of your joy there? He goes on, "That I may gaze on the fair beauty of the Lord" (Ps. 27 : 4).

What do you desire?

My brothers, you would not feel a desire to pray, you would not have any experience of joy or love, unless there were a spark of God's love in your heart. What do you desire? Tell me. Something that you can see and touch, some beauty that entrances your eyes? Have not we all a great love for those who gave their lives for Christ? When you remember them does not your heart overflow with emotion? But what is it that we love in them? The sight of legs and arms torn apart by wild beasts? Nothing could be more repulsive to the outward eye, nothing more beautiful to the inner. You see a beautiful boy who steals. You are repelled, but by what? He is a beautiful creature, comely and fresh; but, when you hear that he is a thief, your whole soul revolts. On the other hand there is an old man, bent double, hobbling along on a stick, his face all rough and wrinkled. There is nothing pleasing in such a sight. Someone tells you how good he is. You love him at once and want to throw your arms round his neck.

The question for us, my brothers, is what we really want. Do we really desire the things that God has promised us? What is the kingdom of our desire, our promised land? Do we want the things of this world?

If that is the reward we want for serving God, then we are still under the Law—and for that very reason we shall find that we cannot keep the Law. When you see all the good things of the world falling into the lap of those who do nothing to please God, do you slacken your pace and say to yourself, "I am always trying to serve God, I go to church every day and wear out my knees in prayer, yet I am always ailing,while those who murder and steal are in the pink of health and lack for nothing. They are the lucky ones"? So that is what you want God to give you, is it? And God's grace had come so close to you. If God gives you His grace so freely, be as generous with your love as He is with His gifts. Do not love God for a reward. Let Him alone be your reward. Let the prayer of your heart be "One thing I have desired . . ." There is no danger of getting tired of that; God's beauty is so wonderful that the more you live with it the more you will hunger for it. It gives you full satisfaction, and yet you can never have enough. If you do not get enough to eat you are hungry; if you get too much you lose your appetite. But there is something that is not hunger and not satiety, a something too wonderful for words to express, which God gives us. We do not know what to call it, but we know it when we get it.

CHAPTER FOUR

THE FOURTH DISCOURSE

Why was Jesus Christ Baptized?

"And I knew Him not; but that He should be manifested to Israel, for this cause came I baptizing with water". Why was John sent to baptize with water? He tells us—"that Christ might be manifested to Israel". Had John's baptism any permanent value? If it had it would still be performed as a preliminary to Christian baptism. But the object of John's baptism was, as he said, simply that Christ should be manifested to God's people Israel. John's task was to prepare the Master's way by baptizing in the waters of repentance—until the Master came. When he recognized the Master, the work of preparing the road was done, because to those who receive Him the Master is Himself the way. So the baptism of John was a temporary thing.

In what light did the Master then manifest Himself? In His humility, for He, the Master, accepted the baptism of His servant. If you ask me, What need had the Lord to be baptized? I ask you, What need had the Lord to be born? What need had He to be crucified? What need had He to die? What need had He to be buried? If He came to humble Himself in these ways, why should He not humble Himself by accepting baptism at the hand of a servant?

What was the reason for it? That we should not be ashamed to accept baptism at the hand of the Master. A very relevant point for us, my friends. He knew that there would be many people on the border of the Church, not yet baptized, but living good lives. We can think of many such people, living in perfect purity, detached from the world, giving up their possessions, distributing their money to the poor; still unbaptized, but better instructed in the truths of salvation than many a Christian. Is there not a danger of such a one saying to himself, "What more shall I get from baptism? I am better than this or that fellow who has been baptized. They have not done as much as I". He has no liking to submit himself to the same treatment as those to whom he thinks himself superior. But really he has never got rid of his sins, and unless he comes to baptism he never will get rid of them or enter the kingdom of heaven, in spite of all his virtues. That is why the Master Himself came to be baptized by His servant, to be able to say to His proud son who does not like to be treated as one of the common crowd, "However far you may have advanced, however many accomplishments you have acquired, however much grace you may have received, have you more than I? If I went to my servant for baptism, are you ashamed to go to your Master?"

You know quite well that the Master did not come to John to get free from sin. John himself said when he saw Him coming, "You come to me! I should be baptized by you". What was His reply? "Allow me please, that all righteousness may be accomplished" (Matt. 3 : 14, 15). Righteousness means humility. He says in effect, "If I can die for men, should I not be baptized for them?" When He submitted to death at the hands of His unfaithful servants should He not submit to baptism at the hands of a faithful one? If this was the purpose of John's baptism, that the

Master's humility should be revealed, then you might have supposed that only He would have been baptized. But that was not so; multitudes had already been baptized by John. Only when the Master had been baptized did the baptizing stop, for John was then put in prison. It was not fitting that only the Master should be baptized, for then it would have been thought that this baptism was a unique rite only suitable for the Master, a better baptism in fact than the Master Himself would give, since His was to be available for the whole human race. But when others were baptized by John, the Master in His humility could share the baptism of common sinners.

So the Master was baptized by the servant, that other servants might not hesitate to be baptized by the Master.

CHAPTER FIVE

THE SEVENTH DISCOURSE

(On the Sunday when St. Augustine was expounding John's designation of Christ as the Lamb of God there was a very powerful counter-attraction to entice his congregation away, a spectacular pagan festival—procession, music and dancing, ending up with a circus and wild beast show in the town's arena. He is pleasantly surprised to find so many of his flock at their places in church, in fact there seems to be a larger congregation than usual. This, the seventh sermon in the series, is one of the longest. The preacher seems to have deliberately filled it out to keep his people in church until the show outside was over. The pastors of those days had no doubts about the effect of such carnivals on the faith and morals of their flock. With these preliminary explanations we pass on to the more interesting parts of his long discourse.)

True Happiness

We are very happy to find so many here to-day. Your eagerness to come is more than we dared hope for. This is the sort of thing that fills the pastor's heart with joy when he is burdened with work and oppressed with the perils of life—to see in his people love for God, zeal for religion, steady hope and burning devotion.

We have just heard in the reading of the Psalm how the poor and needy cries to God in this world, "Let the poor and needy give praise unto thy name" (Ps. 74 : 21).

The voice we hear in the Psalms, as you ought to know, for I have told you many times, is not the voice of one man, yet it is a single voice—the voice of many faithful people, as many as the grains of wheat among the chaff of the threshing floor, scattered throughout the world, yet a single voice, for all are members of the one Body of Christ; a people poor and needy, who find no joy in what goes on in the world around them. Their sorrow—and their joy too—is a hidden thing, only known to Him who hears their groaning and crowns their hoping.

What the world calls pleasure is a very empty thing. We look forward to it eagerly, but when it comes we cannot hold it. The happiness of to-day is gone to-morrow. Nothing is without change in the life of this world, neither things nor people. Everything changes, flies away and vanishes like smoke—poor miserable men who love such things! For the soul becomes like that which it loves. All flesh is grass, and all its glory is like the flower of grass; the grass dries up, the flower falls, but the Word of God abides for ever (Isa. 40 : 6–8). So take care what you love, if you too wish to abide for ever. You want me to tell you how you can find that abiding Word of God to love it? I will—"The Word was made flesh and dwelt among us".

My dear friends, we are poor and needy; but it is just this poverty that enables us to be sorry for those who think they have everything. Their happiness out there is like the happiness of a madman. We all know how happy a lunatic can be. He laughs away to himself all the time and thinks how unfortunate sane people are. We were once like that—out of our mind, and we were cured by the medicine that comes down from heaven. What we used to love we love no longer. So let us strive in prayer for those who have not found their senses. For *He* can restore them to health too. What is needed is that they should see themselves as they are, and realize that there is nothing there to be satisfied about. They are always looking round for some new show to see, but they do not know how to look in and see themselves. If once they could look inwards, they would see that everything there is wrong. Once we start doing this then our interests change and we want to do different things. The sorrow that we then experience is very much more profitable than what they call pleasure.

I think of our many brothers and sisters who are not here. It is a hard thing that our men should be swept along with the crowd; but it is an even more saddening thing that our women whom neither shame nor modesty restrains from gadding round the streets cannot run a little further to the church. However we must leave them to the Merciful One, who sees all, to cure them of their insanity. But as for us who are here, let us partake of the feast that God has prepared and find our joy in His Word. It is He who has invited us to His Gospel feast. He Himself is our food, the sweetest of all foods— but only to those who have the healthy palate that hungers and thirsts after spiritual things.

The Lamb of God

"On the next day John was standing and two of his disciples, and looking on Jesus as He walked said, Behold the Lamb of God".

He is a Lamb in a very special sense. The disciples on occasion were called lambs: "Behold I send you forth as lambs in the midst of wolves" (Matt. 10 : 16). In a similar way they were called lights: "You are the light of the world" (Matt. 5 : 14), but not in the sense that He was called "the true Light which gives light to everyone that comes into the world". So He is the Lamb in a special sense of the word, the one completely pure Lamb without sin—not because His sin has been washed away but because He never had the slightest stain of sin. Why did John call Him the Lamb of God? Was not John himself as pure as a lamb, holy as a man can be, "the friend of the Bridegroom"? He was indeed; but Jesus was the unique Lamb, because His blood and His alone was to be the price of man's salvation.

My brothers, we believe that we have been bought by the blood of the Lamb and set free. What are we to say about those Christians who are joining in to-day's festival of blood, of the blood of some woman or other? What gratitude is this? What an absurd story they tell! Some woman or other—a gold ornament, they say, was torn from her ear and blood flowed; the gold ornament was placed in the scales, but it was greatly outweighed by the blood. Gold outweighed by blood! What about the blood that weighed more than the whole world?

What kind of Lamb was this that the wolves were scared of Him? What kind of Lamb was this that slew the lion by himself being slain? For it is said that the devil is a lion prowling round and roaring, looking for his prey (1 Pet. 5 : 8). The lion was subdued by the Lamb's blood! You see, we Christians too have our circus and wild beast show. Not the empty shows that are put on to please the eyes of the crowds, but the truth itself shown to the eye of the spirit. You have come together here; do not suppose that God will let you go without showing you something worth seeing. God too has His show and He never disappoints His audience.

You see and clap. You would not applaud unless you saw something worth seeing. This is the greatest show in the world, the lion beaten by the blood of the Lamb, the limbs of Christ taken one by one out of the jaws of the lion and put back into the Body of Christ. Some evil spirit or other has put out a parody of the purchase by blood, knowing that it was by the precious blood of Christ that the whole human race was to be redeemed.

False religion and true

It is worth remembering too, my brothers, that those who deceive others with spells and charms and black magic find it necessary to bring the name of Christ into their charms. They have to add a drop of honey to their poison to make Christians take it; they have to try to make their nasty brew taste nice. That is the only way they can seduce Christians.

It is a great mistake to go and look for Christ in any other place than where He chooses to make Himself known to you. Take Him as He wants you to find Him, and in no other way. Take what He tells you and engrave it on your heart. That is the rampart to protect you from every attack the enemy launches and from every plot he lays. You have nothing to fear; the enemy can only do what he is allowed; he is under the Controlling Power; he may test the good, punish the evil, nothing more. You are afraid—of what? Walk with God your Master, and you are quite safe. No suffering will come to you but what He allows to come, and what does come will be painful correction, but not the punishment that falls upon the lost. He is bringing us up as heirs of an eternal inheritance; are we going to refuse His discipline? He is Himself both our Father and our heritage; we possess Him, ought we not to let

54

Him take charge of our education? Let us accept His discipline and not run off to the quacks and spell-merchants, as soon as our head begins to ache.

My brothers, how can I help being distressed about you? I see these things every day, and what am I to do? Have I not even yet been able to persuade those who are called by Christ's name to trust in Him? Suppose the patient who is doctored with spells dies (lots of people who do these things do die, and lots get better without them)—suppose he dies, the question then is with what mark on his forehead does he go to meet God? He has lost Christ's mark and got the devil's. "Oh no, he says, I can never lose Christ's mark". Do you really think that you can have both marks at the same time? Christ does not agree to share His property; when He has bought it, it is His and no one else's. He paid so high a price to have you all for Himself. And you try to make Him share His property by selling yourself to the devil! "Woe to the heart that looks two ways" (Ecclus. 2 : 12)—one face to God, and one face to the devil! God will not share a house on these terms: He will go forth and leave the devil in sole possession. The Apostle did not speak without cause, "Give no place to the devil" (Eph. 4 : 27).

So then, my brothers, let us recognize the Lamb and the price that was paid for us. "John was standing with two of his disciples"—two disciples of John who was content to be the friend of the Bridegroom, who wanted nothing for himself, only that he might bear witness to the truth. Did he want to keep his disciples and not lose them to the Master? On the contrary; he deliberately pointed them to Him whom they should follow. They were inclined to regard John as the Lamb. But John says, "Why are you staying with me? I am not the Lamb. The Lamb is there. I told you before, I tell you now, 'Behold the Lamb of God'." And what will the Lamb do for us? He has told them: "Behold the Lamb of God that takes away the sin of the world". The two who had been with John left him when they heard this and followed the Lamb.

Staying with Jesus

"The two disciples heard him speaking and followed Jesus. Jesus turned and seeing them following him said: What are you looking for? They said, Rabbi (which means Master), where do you live?"

They did not follow Him this time with the intention of staying with Him for ever. That would happen when He called them to leave their boats and said, "Come after me and I will make you fishers of men" (Matt. 4 : 19). On this occasion they followed Him, not with the intention of never leaving Him, but just of seeing where He lived. They were doing what the Scripture told them: "If thou seest a man of understanding, get thee betimes unto him, and let thy foot wear out the steps of his doors" (Ecclus. 6 : 36).

He showed them where He lived. They came and were with Him. What a happy day they had! What a wonderful night! Have we any means of finding out what they heard from the lips of the Master? Yes, there is a way. We must do some building in our own hearts, and make a house where He can come and we can sit at His feet and listen to His teaching. "And He said, Come and see. And they came and saw where He stayed and they remained with Him that day. It was about the tenth hour".

The Christ

"Andrew the brother of Simon Peter was one of the

two who heard from John and followed Him. He finds
his own brother Simon, and says to him, We have
found the Messiah, which means Christ". Messiah is
Hebrew; Christ is Greek; our word is "anointed". He is
called Christ because He is anointed. His anointing was
unique, the special and incomparable anointing. We
Christians are also anointed ones, but our anointing
is secondary, derived from His. This is spoken of in the
Psalm: "Wherefore God, even thy God, anointed
thee with the oil of gladness above thy fellows" (Ps.
45 : 7). His "fellows" are all the saints, but He is the
Saint of saints, the unique Christ.

The Rock

"And he brought him to Jesus. Jesus looked on him
and said, You are Simon the son of John, you shall
be called Cephas, which translated becomes Peter, the
Rock". There is nothing remarkable in the Master
knowing Simon's father's name. Before the world was,
He knew the names of all His saints and arranged for
their lives. The remarkable thing is that He changed his
name and turned Simon into Peter. Peter means rock,
and the Church is a rock. So the name Peter signifies
the Church. Who can have any security unless he
builds on the rock? The Master Himself taught this:
"He who hears my words and does them, I will compare him to a sensible man who builds his house on
rock. The rain comes down, the floods come up, the
wind blows, the full force beats on that house, and it
does not fall, for it has its foundations on rock. He who
hears my words and does not do them [Each one of us
would do well to take warning from this], I will compare him to a foolish man who built his house on sand.
Down came the rain, up came the floods, the wind

blew, all the force broke on the house and it fell, and the ruin was great" (Matt. 7 : 24–27).

What is the use of a man coming into the Church if he is going to build on sand? There are two ways of building. He who hears and does builds on rock, he who hears and does not do builds on sand. What about those who will not even hear? Are they safe because they have built nothing? They are completely exposed to the rain, flood and wind which will sweep them away before even touching the houses. There is only one safe course, to build a house and build it on rock. If you prefer to hear and do nothing, you are building in a fashion, but you are building a ruin. When the storm of temptation comes, it will destroy the house and sweep you away with the debris. If you refuse to hear, you have no protection against temptation at all. So hear and do; this is the only means to health. How many this very day, as a result of hearing and not doing have been swept away in the flood of this carnival. Each year, at this carnival, like a river in spate the flood rushes down the watercourse, and soon all is dry again; but woe to those who have been carried away by the waters. My dear friends, you must understand that unless you both hear and do, you will not build upon rock nor live up to the great name on which the Master set His seal. The lesson of that name was meant for you. If Simon had been called Peter from the first, the mystery of the Rock would never have been brought to your notice so forcibly, and you would have thought that the name was a mere coincidence, not God's intention. He let him have another name to start with, so that by the change of name He might bring home the living reality of the mystery.

I have kept you rather long to-day—deliberately,

until the dangerous time is over. I suppose they have finished their folly by now. Meanwhile, my brothers, we have enjoyed the feast that really makes us whole, and it only remains for us to spend the rest of the Lord's Day in that holy joy, and see how different that holy joy is from the imitation article. Revulsion makes our heart sad. Sadness of heart drives us to prayer. If we pray, let us trust that our prayer will be heard; and answered prayer will mean the winning of their souls.

CHAPTER SIX

THE EIGHTH DISCOURSE

The Miracle at Cana

When we understand what God is always doing, we have no difficulty about believing the miracle that our Master Jesus Christ did when He turned water into wine. What He did at the wedding feast to the water He had poured into the jars is exactly the same as He does year by year in the vineyards. What the servants poured into the jars was changed into wine by the operation of the Master: what the clouds pour down is transformed into wine by the same Master. We do not think that what happens every year is a miracle; we have seen it too often; yet it is really a very much greater miracle than what happened in the water jars. When anyone really thinks of what God does in the world of nature, how He directs and controls every process, he cannot but be overwhelmed by the wonder of the miracle he sees. He holds a little seed in his hand —what force is latent in that little grain! It is stupendous, terrifying.

Most men are so busy with other things that they have lost the power of seeing God in His works, and consequently the desire to worship the Creator every day. That is why God sometimes does things which are out of the ordinary course of nature. He wants men, heavy with sleep, to wake up and realize that He is there. He raises the dead, everyone is amazed: hundreds of babies are born every day, no one pays the slightest attention. Yet which is the more wonderful, to create life that was not there before, or to bring back to life something that had already existed? God the Father of our Master Jesus Christ made all things by His Word; later He worked further miracles through that Word incarnate, made man for us. What was done by Jesus as God is no less wonderful than what He did as man. Earth, sky and sea, all the beauty above, all the profusion beneath, all the abundant life that dwells in the waters—everything that draws our eyes is the work of Jesus as God. If the Spirit of Him who made it lives in our hearts, then we are able to see it all in this light and are drawn to give Him glory. It is wrong when we look at the works in such a way as to turn away from the Worker, when we face the creation and turn our backs on the Creator.

So much for the things that we can see because they come within the range of our eyes. But what of the things that we cannot see, the angels, the "Principalities, Powers and Dominions", all in fact who live in the "heavenly places" beyond the world? All these are out of the range of sight, though angels have when necessary showed themselves to men. Did not God create them all through His Word, that is, through His Son, our Master Jesus Christ?

Then, what about life, the living principle in man, that expresses itself through the physical organism, a most amazing thing if you think about it? Who made it? God of course. How did He make it? Like everything else, through His Son. Even animals have a living something in them which regulates their physical structure, that uses their bodily organs, sees with their eyes, hears with their ears, tastes with their palate, exercises in short the proper functions of each organ.

You cannot see this principle of life, but you can be lost in wonder at what it does.

The animal world is wonderful enough, but man gives us far more to think about, for God has endowed him with the ability to know his Creator, the power of appreciating the difference between good and evil, of choosing between right and wrong. Then think of what man is able to do—he brings the whole natural order under his control, plots it out, organizes it, founds states, makes laws, establishes customs, develops cultures —all this is done by the mysterious living power in man, something that eye can never see. Take life away and there is nothing but a corpse. It is this mysterious living principle and nothing else that keeps the body from dissolving and rotting away. Life holds the physical organism together. This is true both of men and animals. But the powers of man's mind are the more wonderful, especially when they have been renewed after the image of their Creator in which they were first created (Col. 3 : 10).

There is something still more wonderful to come. What will this living power be able to do when "This corruptible puts on incorruption and this mortal puts on immortality"? (1 Cor. 15 : 53–54.) If it can do so much now, what will it be able to do through the spiritual body after the resurrection? We are lost in wonder as we consider the mysterious life in man, invisible indeed, but comprehensible. This too is the work of Jesus Christ, the Word of God. "All things were made by Him, and without Him nothing was made".

When Jesus as God has done all these things, is it at all strange that as Man He should turn the water into wine? When He became man, He did not lose His divine status, He added to Himself the nature of man; He did not suffer the loss of the nature of God. The Person who worked this miracle was the same Person who did all the other things. The wonder is not that He did it, but that He did it as Man among men in order to remake us completely. It is this that draws our love.

The Bridegroom and the Bride

There is also something very significant for us in the event itself. He had, we may suppose, good cause to go to the wedding. Quite apart from the miracle, there is a deep significance and a mysterious power in the episode. We must knock if we would have the door opened. We have to drink the unseen wine and be filled with its joy; for we are just water at first and He turns us into wine. We who had no sense of taste receive from Him the delicate sensibility that belongs to faith. It is this spiritual taste which enables us to understand what took place at that miracle and so give glory and praise to God and respond in love to His compelling compassion.

The Master was invited to the wedding and came. When we remember that it was for a marriage that He came into the world, we cease to be surprised at finding Him at that house on the wedding day. He came into the world to find a bride, so of course He came for a wedding. What did Paul say? "I have betrothed you to one man to present you as a pure virgin to Christ". He has a fear that the purity of Christ's bride may be spoilt by the craft of the devil. "I am afraid," he said, "that as the serpent corrupted Eve by his subtlety, so your hearts may be corrupted from the simplicity and purity that is in Christ" (2 Cor. 11 : 2, 3). So

Christ has a bride; He bought her with His blood and gave her the pledge of the Holy Spirit (2 Cor. 1 : 22). He rescued her from being a slave to the devil, "He died for her transgressions, He rose again for her justification" (Rom. 4 : 25). What bridegroom ever gave his bride such gifts? Men search the world for jewellery—gold, silver, gems, horses, slaves, estates—but who ever gave his own blood? For if any were to give his blood, there would be no one left to marry the bride. But the Master fearlessly faced death, and gave His blood for her who would be His after His resurrection, whom indeed He had already united to Himself in the womb of the virgin. For the Word was the bridegroom and mankind the bride, and the two joined together were one, Son of God and Son of man. When He became the Head of the Church, that womb of the Virgin Mary became His bridechamber, as the Scripture foretold: "And He came forth as a bridegroom out of His chamber, and rejoiced as a giant to run his course" (Ps. 19 : 5). As a bridegroom He came forth from His chamber, and so came, invited, to this marriage.

CHAPTER SEVEN

THE ELEVENTH DISCOURSE

You must be born again

My dear friends; I suppose you have noticed how
very appropriate are the words which we have come to
in our reading of John's Gospel: "Unless a man is
born again of water and the Spirit he will not see the
kingdom of God". This is just the time when we have
to speak very clearly to you who have not yet been
baptized, who believe in Christ after a fashion, but have
not got rid of the burden of your sins. You will never
see the kingdom of God with a pack of sins on your
back. They must be disposed of before you can reign
with Christ. They can never be got rid of unless you are
born again of water and the Holy Spirit. My one subject to-day must be to persuade the slothful how
necessary it is that they should hurry to unload their
burden. If they had a load of stone or wood on their
backs, or even something valuable like corn, wine or
bullion, they would go as fast as possible to the place
where they could put it down. But when the load is
their own sin, they show no inclination to make any
haste. You must run to get rid of that burden, it is
crushing you, drowning you.

We have just read this: "When Jesus was in Jerusalem
at the Passover, on the day of the festival, many
believed on His name, seeing the signs He was doing".
Note what comes next: "Jesus did not trust Himself to

them". They believed on His name, but He did not trust Himself to them. Very strange, and even more so when we remember who it was who refused to trust Himself. He was the Son of God who was completely responsible for His own actions; He was born because He willed to be born, He suffered because He wished to suffer. "I have power to lay down my life, and I have power to take it again: no one takes it from me, but I lay it down of myself, that I may take it up again" (Jn. 10 : 18). Why did Jesus, when such power was His, refuse to trust Himself to them? "Because He knew all, and there was no need for Him to be told about another's character, for He Himself knew what was in man". The workman knows the capacity of the thing he has made better than the thing itself. The Creator knows what is in man in a way that the creature can never know. Take the example of Peter who had no idea about his own character when he said, "I will go with you even to death". But the Lord knew what was in the man: "Verily, verily, I say to you, before the cock crows you will deny me three times" (Matt. 26 : 34, 35). Thus we see that Peter did not know what was in himself; but the Creator knew what was in man. Many believed on His name, but Jesus did not trust Himself to them. Perhaps we shall find the key to this perplexing problem in what follows.

Nicodemus

"There was moreover a man of the Pharisees, Nicodemus by name, a ruler of the Jews. He came by night and said to Him, Rabbi, we know you are a teacher sent from God, for no one could do the signs that you do unless God were with him". Nicodemus was then one of those who had believed on Him, because they saw the signs and wonders that He did. Jesus answered and said, "Verily, I say unto you, except a man be born again he cannot see the kingdom of God". The people Jesus trusted Himself to were those who had been born again. The others who believed on Him and were not trusted—just consider them. They were rather like our catechumens. You ask a catechumen, "Do you believe on Christ?" He will answer, "Yes," and make the sign of the Cross, for he has been signed with the Cross and is not ashamed of the crucified Lord.[1] He has believed on His name. But if we go on to ask, Do you "eat the flesh of the Son of man and drink His blood?", he will not understand what we are talking about, for Jesus has not yet trusted Himself to him.

Nicodemus, being one of these, came to the Master, but he came by night. That is important. He came to the Master—by night; he came to the Light, but he came in darkness. Those who have been born of water and of the Spirit hear these words from the Apostle: "You were once darkness, but are now light in the Lord. Walk as children of the Light" (Eph. 5 : 8); and again "We belong to the day, so we should be sober" (1 Thess. 5 : 8). Those who have been reborn formerly belonged to the night and now belong to the day. They were darkness, now they are light. Now Jesus trusts Himself to them, and they no longer come to Him by night like Nicodemus. They no longer look for the light in the dark. They now acknowledge their faith publicly; and Jesus has come to them and done His healing work in them, for He said, "If a man does not

---

[1] Signing with the sign of the Cross was one of the ceremonies, not of baptism, but of the admission of catechumens.

eat my flesh and drink my blood he has no life in him" (Jn. 6 : 53).

Catechumens have received the sign of the Cross on their foreheads; this means that they have entered the service of a great house. That is no small thing, but it is not enough. They must pass from being servants to being sons. When did the Israelites start to eat the manna? When they had crossed the Red Sea. The Apostle tells us what the Red Sea means: "I would not have you ignorant, brethren, that all our fathers were under the cloud, and all passed through the sea, and all were baptized by Moses in the cloud and in the sea" (1 Cor. 10 : 1, 2). The sea was the symbol, baptism is the reality. In baptism Christ brings those who believe in Him across the sea, drowning the sins that try to follow them like the Egyptians in the waters.

The Bread from Heaven

What did they cross the sea to get? Manna. What is manna? Christ tells us: "I am the Living Bread that comes down from heaven" (Jn. 6 : 51). Believers who have crossed the Red Sea are fed on manna. But why the *Red* Sea? The sea signifies Christ's baptism, and it is red because that baptism is offered to God through the blood of Christ. And that baptism brings men to the manna. Manna is very important. Those who have not yet been baptized know how God rained manna down on His people Israel. They do not know what is the gift that is given to Christians alone. Let them be ashamed of their ignorance. Let them cross the Red Sea and feed on the manna, so that, as they have believed on the name of Jesus, He too may trust Himself to them.

New Birth

You should consider very carefully, my brothers, how the man who came by night reacted to the words of Jesus. He had come to Jesus, it is true; but he had come by night, he was still in the darkness of ordinary human life. He had come to the Master, "the light that lightens every man who comes into the world", and he could not understand what He was saying. The Master said, "Unless a man be born again, he will not see the kingdom of God". Nicodemus said to Him, "How can a man be born when he is old?" Christ spoke on the spiritual level, Nicodemus heard on the human level. He could hear only on the level of his own human experience, because he had not risen to the new level of Christ. He was on the old level because he did not perceive that the Man who was talking to him had come on a new level to lift men up to it. We shall find in the Gospel another case like that of Nicodemus. When Jesus the Master had said, "Unless a man eat my flesh and drink my blood, he has no life in him", even those who had accepted Him as their master found this too much for their faith and said among themselves, "This is a hard saying, who can hear it?" They actually thought that Jesus meant that they could cook Him like meat and eat Him. They were revolted by His words, left Him and had nothing more to do with Him. Then we read: "The Lord remained with the twelve. They said to Him, They have finished with you. He said to them, Do you also want to go away?" (Jn. 6 : 66, 67) He wanted them to see that they were completely dependent upon Him, and not He on them. Do not suppose that you are conferring a favour on Christ by becoming a Christian. He is not the least influenced by that sort of thing. If you have become a Christian it is greatly to your advantage; but Christ does not lose anything if you do not. Listen to the Psalmist: "I have said to the Lord, Thou art my God, my goods are nothing to Thee" (Ps. 16 : 2). That is, "You are my God, because you have no need of my goods". If you are without God, it is your loss. If you are with God, God does not become greater. He is not greater for having you, but you are less from not having Him. Grow in Him; but never imagine that He loses anything if you withdraw yourself from Him. If you come to Him, He makes you new: if you leave Him, you wither away. He is just the same, whether you hold to Him or desert Him. So He said to His disciples, "Do you want to go away?" Peter, the Rock, answered as the spokesman of them all, "Master, to whom shall we go? You have the words of eternal life". He had on his lips the true taste of the flesh of Christ. Then the Master explained to them that they should not interpret His words in a material sense: "It is the Spirit that gives life, the flesh does not help at all. The words which I have spoken are spirit and life" (Jn. 6 : 54–69).

Nicodemus who came to Him by night could not appreciate this "spirit and life" at all. Jesus said, "Unless a man be born anew, he will not see the kingdom of God". He, not yet having that taste of the flesh of Christ, took it in a material way: "How can a man, when he is old, be born again? Can he re-enter his mother's womb and be born?" He only knows one birth, the one that had its origin in Adam and Eve. He knew nothing as yet of the birth that springs from God and the Church. He only knew of the parents who had brought him into the world to die. He knew nothing of the Parents who would give him new birth to live. He knew of fathers and mothers who produce heirs to succeed them. He knew nothing of the Father and Mother who never die and produce children who are to be with them for ever. Whereas there are two births, he only knew of one. One is of the earth, the other of heaven; one is of the flesh, the other of the Spirit; one is finished by death, the other never dies; one is the work of man and woman, the other of God and His Church. But both are alike in this, that neither can happen twice. Nicodemus understood this correctly about birth in the flesh; you should not fail to understand the same about birth in the Spirit. As birth according to Adam cannot be repeated, so neither can birth according to Christ. There cannot be a second birth from the womb, nor can there be a second baptism.

CHAPTER EIGHT

THE TWELFTH DISCOURSE

Son of God and Son of Man

"No one has ascended into heaven except He who descended from heaven, the Son of Man who is in heaven". He was both on earth and in heaven, as man here, as God there and indeed everywhere else besides. Born of a mother, yet not leaving His Father. He is twice a Son, a Son as God, and a Son as man. In the former sonship He made us, in the latter He remade us. We are amazed at both, first a Son with no mother and then a Son with no father. So there is an earthly birth and a heavenly birth. Of the earthly birth He said, "Destroy this temple and in three days I will raise it up". This was His body of Adam's race, the body that Mary gave Him. Of the heavenly birth He said, "Unless a man is reborn of water and the Spirit he will not see the kingdom of God". Just think of it, my brothers, God decided to be the Son of man, and he desires men to be sons of God. He came down for us, we must go up by Him.

Unity

But He came down and went up alone, for He says, "No one ascended into heaven but He who descended from heaven". Does this mean that those whom He makes sons of God will not go up to heaven? Of course they will; for it has been promised, "They shall be equal to the angels". What does it mean, then, that

72

only He who came down goes up? One alone comes down, one alone goes up; what of the rest? If He alone descended and ascended and no one else, is there any hope for the others? There is, because He came down to unite in and with Himself those who were destined to go up with Him, so that they are no longer many but one. "He did not say 'seeds', but 'seed' as referring to one—and in thy 'seed', which is Christ". So said Paul, and again, "You are Christ's, and if Christ's then Abraham's seed" (Gal. 3 : 16, 29). We are all included in the One; that is what He meant. In the Psalms the singular is often used when many are referred to, and the plural when one is referred to.

All this reminds us of the unity of the Church. Let them beware who hate unity and break men up into parties. Listen to a man who wanted to make all men one, with one foundation and one aim. "Do not make divisions. I planted, Apollos watered, but God gave the increase. Yet the planter is nothing, the waterer is nothing, it is God who gives the increase" (1 Cor. 3 : 6–7). The others said, "I am Paul's, I am of Apollos, I am of Cephas, I am of Christ". Paul said, "Is Christ divided?" (1 Cor. 1 : 12–13). Hold to the One, and you will become one organism, one Man, that One, who having come down from heaven, ascended into heaven.

Death

He came down and died, and by His death delivered us from death. Death killed Him, and in dying He struck death dead. You know, my brothers, that it was through the spite of the devil that death entered into the world. Scripture tells us: "God did not make death, nor does He delight in the death of any living thing.

He created everything that it might live" (Wisdom 1 : 13–14), but by the envy of the devil death entered into the world (Wisdom 2 : 24). It was not by superior force that man was to be brought to drink of the death cup proffered by the devil. The devil had no power to compel, only a deadly ingenuity in persuading. If you had not consented, the devil would have had no way of getting in. It was your own free will, man, that brought you to death. Men are subject to death because their parents were; they are born mortal. But they were not made so. They were made not to die; they came through their own choice into the condition of being subject to death. All men are mortal from Adam; but Jesus is the Son of God, the Word of God, through whom all things were made, the one and only Son equal to the Father; and He became subject to death, because "the Word was made flesh and dwelt among us".

The conquest of Death

So He accepted death, and hanged death on the cross, and those who were subject to death were set free from death. The Master reminds us that this was foreshadowed in something that happened a very long time ago: "As Moses lifted up the serpent in the desert, so the Son of Man must be lifted up, that all who believe in Him may not perish, but have eternal life". A great mystery, as those who take the trouble to read the account will understand. For those who cannot read, or those who have read or heard the story and forgotten it, I will tell it now. When they were in the desert, the people of Israel were plagued with snakes and a large number of them were bitten and died. God sent this plague to rebuke their sin and

74

punish them, because He had a lesson to teach them. In this event there is a mysterious foreshadowing of what was to come; so the Master tells us, lest we should make any mistake in interpreting the incident. Moses was told by the Lord to make a snake of brass and lift it up on a stake in the desert, and then to tell the people that when anyone was bitten by a snake he was to look up at the brass snake on the pole. So it happened. Men were bitten. They looked up and were cured (Num. 21 : 6–9). What is meant by the snakes? They are the sins of men doomed to die. And the serpent lifted up on the post? The death of the Master on the cross. Most fittingly a snake, for death was brought in by a serpent. The bite of the snake kills: the death of the Master gives life. They have to look at the snake in order to render the snake harmless. Most extraordinary. To look at death to take the power out of death. But to look at whose death? The death of Life, if one dare say such a paradoxical thing—the death of Life—yet nothing less is true. Shall we hesitate to put into words what actually happened? I must tell you what the Master in His goodness has done for me. Christ is our life, and Christ hung on the cross. He is our life, and yet He died. What died on the cross? Death died. Life by dying killed death. Life in its fulness swallowed up death. Death was absorbed in the Body of Christ.

In the resurrection we shall sing the song of triumph, "Death, where is thy victory, death, where is thy sting?" (1 Cor. 15 : 54, 55.) Until then, my brothers, we must look up at Christ crucified, in order that we may be healed from sin. That is what the Master meant when He said: "As Moses lifted up the serpent in the desert, so the Son of Man must be lifted up, that no one

who believes in Him may perish, but have eternal life".
As none of those who looked up to the serpent died of the bites, so none who look with faith on the death of Christ shall fail to be healed of the poison of sin. They were healed to go on living in this world; but the Master said, "That they may have eternal life". Here lies the difference between the foreshadowing and the actual event: the shadow gave life in time, the reality gives life in eternity.

Not to judge but to save

"God did not send His Son into the world to judge the world, but that the world might be saved through Him". So He came to do for the sick man what a physician can do. If the patient does not do what the doctor tells him, he is responsible for his own death. Christ came as Saviour of the world, so of course He came not to judge but to save. If you do not want Him to save you, you have judged yourself—Yes, judged yourself, for this is what He said, "He who believes on Him is not judged, but he who does not believe"— What do you expect Him to say?—"is judged"? No, He says, "Has been judged already". The judgment is not yet evident, but it has already been given. The Master knows who belongs to Him. He knows who will attain the crown of heaven and who the fire of hell. He knows the chaff on His threshing floor, and He knows the grain. He knows the wheat, and He knows the tares. He who does not believe has already been judged. Why? "Because he has not believed on the name of the only-begotten Son of God".

Coming to the Light

"This is the judgment, that the light has come into

the world, and men loved the darkness more than the light, because their works were evil". My brothers, whose works did the Master find good? No one's, all were bad. How then could some manage to "do the truth" so as to come to the light? For this is what He goes on to say: "He who does the truth comes to the light, that his works may be made manifest that they are done in God". What is meant by "doing the truth" so as to come to the light, that is, to Christ? And on the other hand what does "loving darkness" mean? We know that He found only sinners when He came; we know that He can cure all sin; we know that the serpent was set up because men were bitten, that is that the Master died for men condemned as wicked and doomed to die; knowing all this, how are we to understand the passage: "This is the judgment, that light came into the world, and men loved darkness better than light, because their deeds were evil"? What does this mean? Whose deeds were good? Did He not come to make the wicked righteous? But what is said is, "They loved darkness rather than light".

That is what He emphasizes. Some loved their sins, some confessed them. Now those who confess their sins and accuse themselves are acting with God. God accuses you of sin; you accuse yourself; then you are co-operating with Him. Distinguish between the man and the sinner. You are called "man"; that is because of the act of God. You are called "sinner"; that is because of your own act. Repudiate what you are responsible for, and so let God save what He is responsible for. Hate what you have done, and love what God does in you. When you begin to detest what you have done, your doing of good works has already begun because you are acknowledging your own works to be bad.

The starting point of good deeds is the confession of bad ones. You are beginning to do the truth, and so you begin to come to the light. Can you not see what "doing the truth" means? Get rid of self-love, self-deception, self-flattery; stop thinking you are good when you are not; and then you have already begun to "do the truth". You are coming to the light, that your works may be manifest that they are done in God. You would never have come to feel that revulsion from sin unless God's light had shone upon you and His truth opened your eyes.

On the other hand, if anyone goes on loving his sins even when he has been told that they are evil, that man hates the light that admonishes him and runs away from it, in order that those sins of which he is so fond may not be shown up as evil. He who "does the truth" denounces his own sins, and does not spare himself, does not pardon himself, but leaves that to God. He confesses what he desires God to pardon, and so comes to the Light and is grateful to the Light for showing him what he should hate in himself. He says to God, "Turn thy face from my sins"; and he says it openly lest he should have to say again, "I know my wrongdoing, and my sin is ever before me" (Ps. 51 : 9, 3). Face for yourself what you do not want God to look at. If you put your sin behind your back, God will bring it round to the front again and set it firmly before your eyes, and that will be when penitence is of no further avail.

My brothers, run lest the darkness catch you (Jn. 12 : 35). Be alive to the issue of your salvation—while there is still time. Let nothing keep you from the worship of God's house or from the Master's work. Let nothing draw you away from continual prayer, nothing deprive you of your regular devotion. Be on the alert while daylight lasts. The light of day is there; Christ Himself is the day. He is ready to forgive, but you must confess. He has punishment ready for those who make excuses for themselves and claim that they are all right, thinking they are something when they are nothing.

If a man lives in the consciousness of the love and mercy of God, he is not content to be free from the great deadly sins—notorious crimes like murder, adultery and theft; he makes an honest acknowledgment of things which might be thought of little importance—sins of speech, sins of thought, lack of self-control in things which are good in themselves. In this way he comes with good deeds to the light. Sins small in themselves, if allowed to continue, become deadly. A river is made up of small drops of water. A grain of sand is a very tiny thing, but sand in bulk is one of the heaviest things there are. Waves pouring over the side can sink a ship, but so can water in the bilge. Slowly but surely it trickles down, and if no one bales it out the ship will founder. A boat has continually to be baled, so we have to keep down the little sins by good deeds; this means by contrition, self-discipline, confessions and forgiving. The path through life is not an easy one; it is full of temptations—when things go well, to pride, when things go wrong, to despair. But remember that God gives you the good things of this life not to spoil you but to encourage you; and the hard things not to punish you but to reform you. Accept the Father's discipline and you will not experience the Judge's punishment. We are always saying these things, and we always must, for it is sound and salutary teaching.

www.ingramcontent.com/pod-product-compliance
Lightning Source LLC
LaVergne TN
LVHW021619080426
835510LV00019B/2655